99 Fun Ideas

for Teaching Bible Verses

by Elizabeth Whitney Crisci

STANDARD PUBLISHING

Cincinnati, Ohio   3072

All Scriptures are from the *King James Version* and the *Holy Bible New International Version,* Copyright 1978 by New York International Bible Society. Used by permission of New York International Bible Society.

Illustrated by Richard Briggs

ISBN 0-87239-869-2

Library of Congress Cataloging in Publication Data

Crisci, Elizabeth W.
    99 fun ideas for teaching Bible verses.

    1. Bible—Memorizing.   I. Title.   II. Title: Ninety-nine fun ideas for teaching Bible verses.
    BS617.7.C75 1985   268'.6   85-2708
    ISBN 0-87239-869-2

Copyright 1985. The STANDARD PUBLISHING Company, Cincinnati, Ohio.
A division of STANDEX INTERNATIONAL Corporation.
Printed in U.S.A.

Contents

Introduction

God's Word is special. It is a light unto my path (Psalm 119:105), it is faithful (119:86), it is settled in Heaven (119:89), it is my meditation all the day (119:97). But that is because I have hidden it in my heart (119:11), and it is part of my life.

I grew up in a day of memorization. I was taught to put the Word of God into my head to keep me from sin, to share with a dying world, to guide me through the valley of the shadow of death.

Pity the young people today who are drifting through Sunday school and youth groups without the foundation of memorized Scripture. They will become adults with a vacuum in their hearts and a blank space in their heads. For some, the false cults, the atheism, or the humanistic philosophy will be free to enter and take root.

Oscar Wilde in *The Importance of Being Earnest* wrote, "Memory is the diary that we all carry with us." What will the next generation carry with it? Family fights? Nuclear threats? Street violence? TV heroes and songs?

The Bible is still alive; it is quick and powerful, and sharper than any two-edged sword (Hebrews 4:12). To learn it need not be drudgery. Indeed, it can be pleasant and even fun. It all depends on the teacher.

99 Fun Ideas for Teaching Bible Verses is not meant to be easy for the teacher; it will be fun and easy for the student. The teacher must put planning time into this part of the lesson preparation if it is to become a vital part of the student's life now and later.

"Study to show thyself approved unto God, a workman that needeth not to be ashamed, rightly dividing the word of truth" (2 Timothy 2:15, *KJV*). "Do your best to present yourself to God as one approved, a workman who does not need to be ashamed and who correctly handles the word of truth" (2 Timothy 2:15, *NIV*).

Elizabeth Whitney Crisci

One: Hidden Words

From your lesson plan, select the verse to be learned for the day and hide each word within a puzzle. The words can be diagonal, horizontal or vertical, up or down, frontwards or backwards. Some words may overlap. Philippians 4:19 is an example.

Copy on a copy machine, typewriter and carbon, or mimeograph one for each student. In a given time limit, they are to circle the words from the verse, then memorize it and say it for the teacher and students.

NEW INTERNATIONAL VERSION

```
A  S  I  H  A  I  R  Z  F  G  C
I  R  I  C  H  E  S  L  N  L  K
Q  B  S  J  A  E  L  I  F  O  S
Y  Y  O  U  R  I  D  K  T  R  B
H  U  Y  B  W  R  N  Y  C  Y  J
N  P  G  G  O  D  E  L  M  I  T
T  W  L  C  E  S  E  P  T  O  S
E  C  C  L  O  U  D  P  X  U  I
E  A  O  Y  A  S  S  U  N  S  R
M  I  M  Q  V  E  F  S  H  I  H
A  N  D  C  X  J  L  D  U  M  C
```

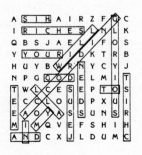

Two: Flannelgraph Card Wipeout

Select the memory verse and print it on card stock, construction paper, or light-weight cardboard—one word to each card. Roughen the back of the construction paper with sandpaper or paste flannelgraph paper to the back of each card so it will adhere to the flannelgraph board.

Place all of the words in the correct order on the flannelgraph board. Have the children read it aloud twice. Then choose a student to come up and remove one word while the children close their eyes. They guess the missing word and repeat the verse. Another student comes and removes a word while the children close their eyes. They guess the missing word and again say the verse. Continue the process until all the words are gone. The class will learn the verse just from the process of guessing missing words and saying the verse.

ALL	SCRIPTURE	IS	GIVEN	BY
INSPIRATION	OF	GOD,	AND	IS
PROFITABLE	FOR	DOCTRINE,	FOR	
REPROOF,	FOR	CORRECTION,	FOR	
INSTRUCTION	IN	RIGHTEOUSNESS.		

2 TIMOTHY 3:16

KING JAMES VERSION

8

Three: Duck, Duck, Verse

The verse of the day is posted in a prominent place. The children sit in a circle, and one person who is *it* goes around the circle tapping each student on the head and saying, "Duck, duck, duck, duck, verse." The one whose head is tapped with "verse" must repeat the verse. That person then becomes *it,* and he/she goes around the circle, tapping the others on the head. Continue this until all have had opportunity to be *it.* Remove the verse from view and start again. This time, the students must say the verse from memory.

The same game may be used to review all the verses from the past month or unit. The *it* can say, "Duck, duck, duck, duck, John 3:16," "Duck, duck, duck, duck, Philippians 4:19," etc. When a child quotes the verse correctly, that child becomes *it.*

Four: Cut-up Contest

Print or type the memory verse on a sheet of paper. Make a copy for each student, then cut each sheet into pieces to make a jigsaw puzzle. The students put the puzzle together, then learn it. The teacher may remove one or two puzzle pieces from each student's puzzle and see if he/she can say the verse.

Option: Make a large puzzle, and glue flannelgraph paper to the back of each piece. Let a student who has memorized the verse put it together as the others watch. Remove different pieces and have the children say the verse.

KING JAMES VERSION

For God so loved the world that He gave His only begotten Son that whosoever believeth in Him should not perish but have everlasting life. John 3:16

This system may be adapted to any age: simple puzzles for first graders, complicated puzzles for older children.

Five: Bible-song Invention

Write a verse out for the students, or have them look it up in their Bibles. Put the words of the verse to a familiar tune and let them sing it a few times. Then say, "Give me the verse without the song!" They will be able to, having learned it without effort.

Romans 3:23
King James Version
Tune: "Farmer in the Dell"
For all have sinned we read
For all have sinned we read
And come short of the glory of God
For all have sinned we read.

Exodus 20:3
New International Version
Tune: "Mary Had a Little Lamb."
You shall have no other gods
Other gods, other gods
You shall have no other gods
Before me.

Revelation 2:10
King James Version
Tune: "Jesus Loves Me."
Be thou faithful unto death
Unto death, unto death
Be thou faithful unto death
And I'll give thee a crown of life.

Matthew 6:12
King James Version
Tune: "O How I Love Jesus."
Forgive us our debts
Forgive us our debts
Forgive us our debts
As we forgive our debtors.

Six: Word Scrambles

Explain to the children the meaning of the memory verse, but do not tell them the words. Then jumble the words for the children to unscramble as a class or as individuals. After using this method a couple of times, let some of the children do the scrambling and see if the others can unscramble their work. Example: Psalm 119:11

KING JAMES VERSION

YTH RWDO HEAV I DIH
NI NEIM EHRAT, AHTT I
GTIHM TNO SNI STINAAG
EHET.

NEW INTERNATIONAL VERSION

I VEAH DEDIHN UYRO
WDRO NI YM AREHT TTHA
I TGHIM TNO ISN
GAANIST UYO.

As the children unscramble the verse, the words will be fixing themselves into their minds. It will then be easy to memorize the verse and say it for the teacher.

Seven: Tape-recorder Learning Spree

Children love to hear themselves on a tape recorder. Take advantage of the desire, and help them learn a verse in the process.

1. Write the verse on a chalkboard or a flash card for all to see and read, or have them read the verse from the Bible.
2. Turn on the tape recorder.
3. Have the class read the verse in unison.
4. Have volunteers read the verse to the class.
5. Rewind and play back the tape.
6. Erase the chalkboard, turn the flash card over, or close Bibles.
7. Ask the class to say the verse from memory.
8. Turn on the tape recorder.
9. Have the class say the verse from memory onto the tape.
10. Ask for volunteers to say the verse onto the tape.
11. Replay the voices on the tape.
12. Ask everybody once again to say the verse from memory.
13. Talk about the meaning of the verse for their lives.

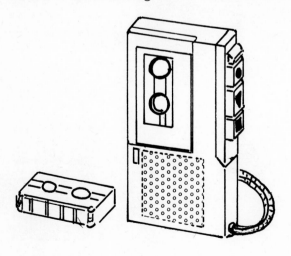

Eight: Verse Crossword

Any memory verse can be adapted to this method. It will take only a few minutes to work it up.

Have the students look up the verse in their Bibles, write it out in order, and memorize it. Advanced students may try to figure out the wording of the verse without looking it up, and check it only after they try to arrange the words in order.

NEW INTERNATIONAL VERSION

Across
1. Honor
2. Preposition: from
4. Speak
5. Definite article
8. The skies
10. Preposition: from
11. Definite article
12. Heavens

Down
1. The Creator
3. Speak
5. Definite article
6. Definite article
7. Possessive form of he
8. Part of body at end of arms
9. Labor

Nine: Not-bored-chalkboard

Before class, print the verse of the day on the chalkboard. Do it as attractively as possible. Use colored chalk, and draw some simple illustrations to call attention to it. But do not mention it until later in the session. At the proper moment, ask, "What is our verse for today?" Let several read it. Then let a child erase one word. The entire class will read through the verse, including the word that is now missing. Choose a student to read it alone. He/she can be the next to erase a word. Continue the process until all the words are missing and the students "read" from their rememberers.

KING JAMES VERSION

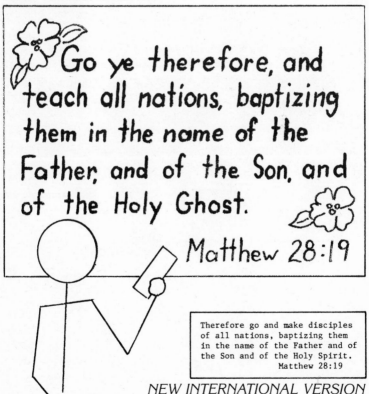

Go ye therefore, and teach all nations, baptizing them in the name of the Father, and of the Son, and of the Holy Ghost. Matthew 28:19

Therefore go and make disciples
of all nations, baptizing them
in the name of the Father and of
the Son and of the Holy Spirit.
                Matthew 28:19

NEW INTERNATIONAL VERSION

15

Ten: Match Ups

Match ups work well for review of verses used during a period of several weeks. On construction paper, print a verse. On a contrasting color, print the Bible reference. The children must match the proper reference with each verse.

KING JAMES VERSION   *NEW INTERNATIONAL VERSION*

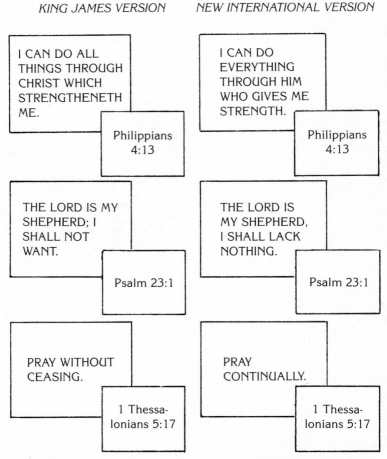

I CAN DO ALL THINGS THROUGH CHRIST WHICH STRENGTHENETH ME.

Philippians 4:13

I CAN DO EVERYTHING THROUGH HIM WHO GIVES ME STRENGTH.

Philippians 4:13

THE LORD IS MY SHEPHERD; I SHALL NOT WANT.

Psalm 23:1

THE LORD IS MY SHEPHERD, I SHALL LACK NOTHING.

Psalm 23:1

PRAY WITHOUT CEASING.

1 Thessalonians 5:17

PRAY CONTINUALLY.

1 Thessalonians 5:17

When a student matches the verses with their proper references, let him/her read it to the class. Every recitation of the verse fixes it more firmly in the mind of the student.

Eleven: Dot-to-dot Verse

Most children are familiar with dot-to-dot work with numbers. To vary the puzzle, use words of the memory verse at each dot. If the children know the verse correctly, the connection of dots will form a picture. Let them study the verse for five minutes before going to work.

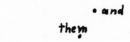

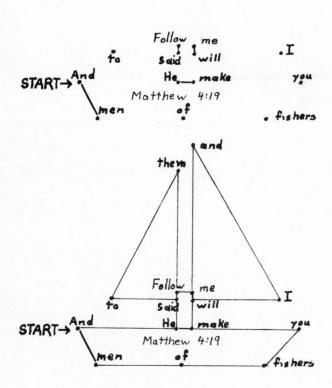

Twelve: Sandbox Words

Put several inches of sand, cornmeal, or kitty litter in a rectangular cake pan or box.

Write each word of the verse on a card. Fasten a popsicle stick to the back of each card. Stand the words in the sand and have the children say the words. Remove a word and have them say the verse. Remove another word and have them say the verse, etc. Mix up the words and let the students put them in the proper order.

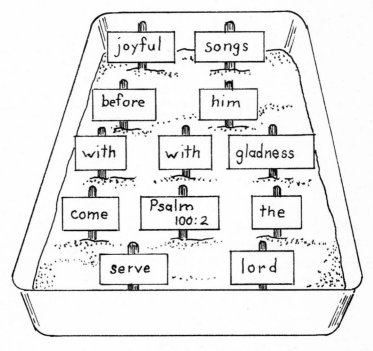

NEW INTERNATIONAL VERSION

Thirteen: Mode Codes

Codes are fun to make and fun to do. Here is a chemistry stencil mode. Example: Philippians 4:13. See page 20 for the code.

NEW INTERNATIONAL VERSION

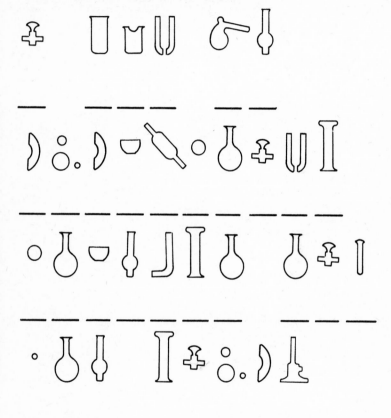

A = ⊔ B = 🌡 C = ⊔ D = 𝒫 E =)

F = ▽ G = ∏ H = ⬭ I = ⊹ J = ◯

K = ◊ L = ◗ M = ▯ N = ⊍ O = ⬭

P = △ Q = ⬭ R = ⊍ S = ⌐ T = ◯

U = ⌐ V = ⊙ W = o X = ⌐ Y = ⬭

Z = ◯

When you have worked out the code, use a copier to reproduce the code for the students. They will have fun as they learn. Vary the codes for special verses.

Fourteen: Roll the Scroll

Give each child a 4¼″ x 11″ sheet of paper and two popsicle sticks or straws. For younger children, print the verse in dotted lines and let them trace over the letters. Older children can copy the verse from their Bibles. Let the children glue the sticks or straws to the ends of the paper to make the scroll. Have the children read the verse. Talk about the meaning of the verse, and teach the chorus of "Trust and Obey" while the glue dries.

KING JAMES VERSION

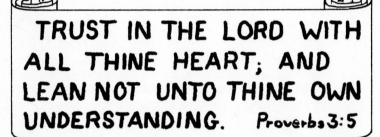

NEW INTERNATIONAL VERSION

When the sticks are dry, have the children roll the scrolls halfway shut and say the verse. Let them roll the scroll almost shut and say the verse again. Then let them completely close it and say it.

21

Fifteen: TV for Me

Find a carton about the size of a portable television—approximately 12" x 12". With a sharp knife, cut out a frame for the screen. Cut a slit on each side from top to bottom.

Let each child or group of children make one 8" x 11" picture frame with the appropriate words. Fasten the frames together to make a long picture strip. Slide the strip through the slits and say the verse. Bring the TV back for review at the end of the month. *Option:* Try making a rebus (pictures to represent words) without the words.

KING JAMES VERSION

NEW INTERNATIONAL VERSION

Sixteen: Overhead Learning

Give each student an overhead transparency and a marker. Let them write the memory verse and draw an appropriate illustration. You may want to make a list of verses (such as the Ten Commandments) and have different children do different verses.

Project the transparencies on a wall or screen. Have the children read the verse and talk about it.

KING JAMES VERSION

IN MY FATHER'S HOUSE ARE MANY MANSIONS: IF IT WERE NOT SO I WOULD HAVE TOLD YOU. I GO TO PREPARE A PLACE FOR YOU.
John 14:2

IN MY FATHER'S HOUSE ARE MANY ROOMS; IF IT WERE NOT SO, I WOULD HAVE TOLD YOU. I AM GOING THERE TO PREPARE A PLACE FOR YOU.
John 14:2

NEW INTERNATIONAL VERSION

Seventeen: Time to Scrape

Give each child a square of heavy paper and a bright color crayon. Have them color the pages with the crayons. (They will need to make the page as dark as possible.) Next, have them color over the page again with a black, dark blue, or brown crayon. Finally, with a sharp point, such as the end of a paper clip, have them scrape-print the words of the verse on the paper so the bright color underneath will show through.

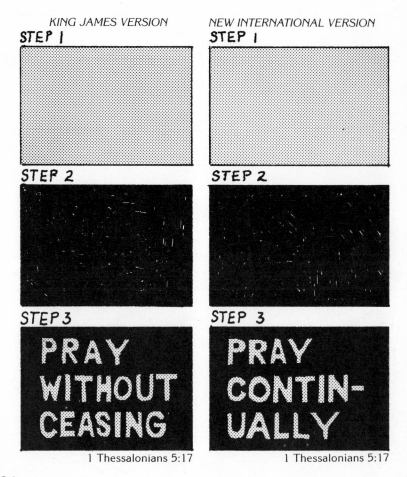

KING JAMES VERSION

STEP 1

STEP 2

STEP 3

PRAY WITHOUT CEASING

1 Thessalonians 5:17

NEW INTERNATIONAL VERSION

STEP 1

STEP 2

STEP 3

PRAY CONTIN-UALLY

1 Thessalonians 5:17

Eighteen: Bible Bridge

To help explain the bridge between sinful man and the Holy God, let the children make a bridge. Give each child a piece of paper or cardboard and some markers or crayons. (You may want to make a large bridge for the children to see.) Have extra pieces of paper and tape available for attaching the overlays.

KING JAMES VERSION

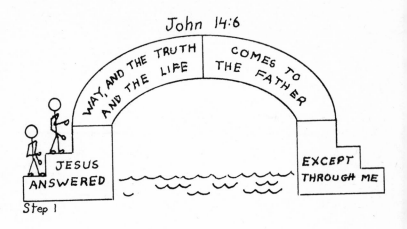

Nineteen: Ball Throw

This Bible memory scheme may be used with small children or older ones. Write the verse on a chalkboard or chart. Have the children read it together twice. Throw a soft rubber or sponge ball to a child and say the first word of the verse. The student must say the first and second words of the verse as he returns the ball to the teacher. The teacher says the first three words of the verse as he throws the ball to a different student. The student says the first four words as he returns the ball to the teacher, etc. The students must always return the ball to the teacher; otherwise, the game gets too rough. This keeps the teacher in control. After several times of saying the verse, erase the verse and have the students then say the words from memory.

With preschool children, you may want to sit on the floor, roll the ball, and have each child say the Bible words as he returns the ball to you.

Twenty: Mirror Verse

Write the verse for the week backwards. If you have difficulty, use a mirror to figure out the letters. Give each child a copy, and let them write it correctly. Have ready related verses for them to copy from their Bibles, then write the verses in mirror writing. You may want to have small mirrors available for the children to use. (An easy way to make backward copies is to put carbon paper in wrong side up.)

KING JAMES VERSION

IF WE CONFESS OUR SINS, HE IS FAITHFUL AND JUST TO FORGIVE US OUR SINS, AND TO CLEANSE US FROM ALL UNRIGHTEOUSNESS.
I John 1:9

Twenty-one: Melodic Chairs

Set the classroom chairs in a line, every other one in the opposite direction. On two chairs, place a card that says MEMORY VERSE CHAIR. Play a cassette or the piano as the children march around the chairs. When the music stops, the two sitting in the "verse" chairs must say the memory verse. For the first few times, they may read the verse from the chalkboard. Then begin erasing a word of the verse each time they go around and continue until nothing is left. If they can say the verse, they remain in the game. If they cannot say the verse, they must drop out.

NEW INTERNATIONAL VERSION

If you love me, you will obey what I command.

John 4:15

MEMORY VERSE CHAIRS

Twenty-two: Miniature Bible Verse

Another variation of memory work can consist in writing the verse as small as possible. Let each child try, with a very sharp pencil, to put the verse on a one-inch square paper. As they try, they will be learning. Then they can try to read someone else's verse. Bring several magnifying glasses to help. If the letters cannot be read with the magnifying glass, they do not count.

Have a sample ready. Let the children read it. Place it farther away from them and let them read it. Soon, they will be "reading" it from memory. Our example is Proverbs 15:1.

Twenty-three: Fill in the Vowels

Write all of the consonants of the words in the verse, but leave the vowels blank. Let the children fill in the blanks. After they have read the verse a couple of times, reverse the process: write only the vowels, and have them add the consonants.

KING JAMES VERSION

BL__SS__D __R__ TH__
P__R__ __N H__ __RT:
F__R TH__Y SH__LL
S__ __ G__D.
M__TTH__W 5:8

__ __E__ __E__ A__E __ __E
__U__E I__ __EA__ __:
__O__ __ __ __E__ __ __A__ __
__EE __O__ .
__A__ __ __E__ 5:8

NEW INTERNATIONAL VERSION

BL__SS__D __R__ TH__
P__R__ __N H__ __RT,
F__R TH__Y W__LL
S__ __G__D.
M__TTH__W 5:8

__ __E__ __E__ A__E __ __E
__U__E I__ __EA__ __,
__O__ __ __ __E__ __I__ __ __
__EE __O__ .
__A__ __ __E__ 5:8

31

Twenty-four: Buzzer Fun

Every class needs a buzzer. It is great for "quiet down" instructions, for "begin your work" instruction, and for memory fun.

Here are two ways to use a kitchen timer. Set it at two minutes and let the students work on the verse. Anyone who can say the verse to the teacher before the timer sounds receives a sticker, a check mark, or some other form of recognition.

Another way to use the timer is to pass the verse around the circle of students. When the timer goes off, whoever has the verse reads it to the others. After three or four times, a blank piece of paper is substituted for the verse. When the timer goes off, the person who has the paper "reads" it from memory.

KING JAMES VERSION

Twenty-five: Magnet-board Time

Children and young people are fascinated with magnets. Why not put them to work in memorizing verses? You will need a metal tray, a stove protector, or any sheet of metal. Cover it with thin paper and print "YOUR VERSE" at the top if desired.

For small children, find pictures to illustrate the verse. For readers, write the words on cards. Attach magnets to the back of each card, and place the cards on the board in any fashion: mixed up, in order, a phrase at a time, etc.

Magnets and rubber magnetic strips are available in bookstores and craft departments. They are inexpensive and reusable. A good way for review is to type a complete verse on a small card and glue a magnet on the back. Students may take the cards home and place them on their refrigerators for the entire family to see and learn.

NEW INTERNATIONAL VERSION

SHOUT WITH JOY TO GOD ALL THE EARTH PSALM 66:1

Twenty-six: Bible-verse Mural

A mural is a thinking project children do not soon forget. Select a verse with phrases and action. Get a long piece of shelf paper, newsprint, or tablecover roll and divide it into equal sections with a pencil line. Print a phrase for each child or group to illustrate, and give them time to work on it. They may use crayons, felt markers, scraps of construction paper, or 3-D materials: cloth, beads, etc., for a collage.

NEW INTERNATIONAL VERSION

Twenty-seven: Verse A-la-macaroni

Buy some alphabet macaroni or cereal and let the children find the letters, glue them to a backing, and learn the verse. They may take the project home as a review, a reminder, and a family remembrance.

For beginning readers, presort the letters into divided trays such as egg cartons. A construction-paper triangle is a good stand-up design. Make three dotted lines as illustrated. Glue the letters on while it is still flat, then fold and glue the triangle.

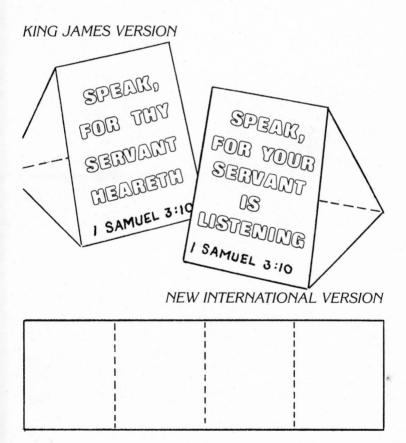

KING JAMES VERSION

SPEAK, FOR THY SERVANT HEARETH
I SAMUEL 3:10

SPEAK, FOR YOUR SERVANT IS LISTENING
I SAMUEL 3:10

NEW INTERNATIONAL VERSION

Twenty-eight: Letter Setter

Cut construction paper into one-inch squares and, with a felt maker, put an alphabet letter on each square. Make enough for everyone to do the particular verse chosen. (You may eliminate Q, Z, X, and other letters that won't be used.) Write the verse on the chalkboard, and put the letters upside down on a table. At a signal, each child takes six letters and goes to work. Any letters they do not need they may place back in the pile upside down, and take two more letters. If and when they use all their letters, they may take six more. The first one to spell out the entire verse is the winner. For additional fun and learning, erase part of the words, and eventually all of them.

KING JAMES VERSION

FOR I KNOW THAT MY REDEEMER LIVETH. Job 19:25

NEW INTERNATIONAL VERSION

I KNOW THAT MY REDEEMER LIVES. Job 19:25

Twenty-nine: Spinner Game

From cardboard and a paper fastener make a spinner game like the one pictured below. Let the students take turns spinning and performing the job indicated: read the verse from the board; quote the reference; say the last half of the verse from memory; say the first half of the verse from memory; say last week's verse from memory; or say the entire verse from memory. If a student fails, he/she becomes a third of a glob. The game can stop before anyone becomes a whole glob, or the globs may stand on one foot until the game ends.

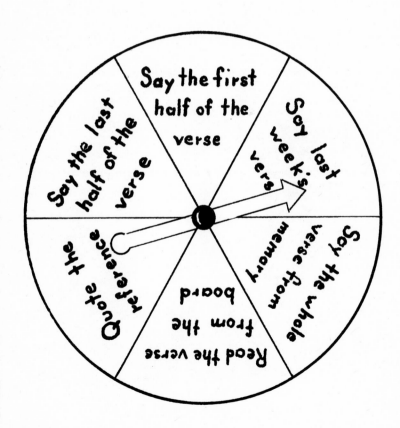

Thirty: Hide Me if You Can

Write the verse on the chalkboard or a chart. Have the class read it together several times to become familiar with the words. Then hand a small Bible-shaped card with the verse written on it to a child to hide. One child must leave the room until the hiding place is selected. When the child is brought back in, he searches the room, looking for the verse. The class will say the verse softly if the student is far away, more loudly as he gets closer. When the student finds the card, he tries to say the verse from memory. If he can, he gets to choose the next hunter and hides the card while the other student is out of the room. Before long, everyone will know the verse, and you will need to start a new one!

KING JAMES VERSION

Thirty-one: Back Talk

As each student arrives, place a card with part of the verse for the day on his back. Several children may have the same words. Anyone may ask anyone else any question he wants to ask about the words on his back so long as the question can be answered by "yes" or "no." Allow five minutes for the game.

Be sure the words are said often enough for everyone to learn the verse.

NEW INTERNATIONAL VERSION

Thirty-two: Abraham and Sarah

This game consists of a group of form questions that lead to the reciting of the memory verse. If the verse for the week is John 3:36, the conversation would go like this:

Abraham: Sarah, where are you?

Sarah: Here I am, Abraham.

Abraham: What do you say, Sarah?

Sarah: I say John 3:36, Abraham.

Abraham: How do you say John 3:36, Sarah?

Sarah: I say it correctly, Abraham.

Abraham: Then say it, Sarah.

Sarah: "He that believeth on the Son hath everlasting life: and he that believeth not the Son shall not see life; but the wrath of God abideth on him." John 3:36,* Abraham *(KJV)*

Abraham: Very good, Sarah. Will you see if Isaac knows our verse?

At this point, Sarah takes the lines of Abraham, and Isaac takes the lines of Sarah. There may also be a Jacob, a Joseph, a Rebecca, a Rachel, etc., until everyone has a turn. For the first run-through, the verse can be printed on the board. After each conversation, erase one phrase of the verse until there is nothing left and the students are saying it from memory. The students should be sure they say the words in the conversation exactly as planned. The participants waiting for their turns should be listening to make sure there are no mistakes. Each mistake makes the student a fourth of a glob.

* "Whoever believes in the Son has eternal life, but whoever rejects the Son will not see life, for God's wrath remains on him." *(NIV)*

Thirty-three: Slide for Memory

Copy the exercise below (without the answers) for all students. Tell them the key to finding the verse is to slide two letters backward. For instance, E = C and Q = O. Older students can do the exercise on their own. You may need to give the code to younger children. C = A, D = B, E = C, F = D, G = E, H = F, I = G, J = H, K = I, L = J, M = K, N = L, O = M, P = N, Q = O, R = P, S = Q, T = R, U = S, V = T, W = U, X = V, Y = W, Z = X, A = Y, B = Z, 13 = 11, 30 = 28.

KING JAMES VERSION

‾ ‾ ‾ ‾   ‾ ‾ ‾ ‾   ‾ ‾ ,   ‾ ‾ ‾
e q o g   w p v q   o g   c n n

‾ ‾ ‾ ‾ ‾ ‾   ‾ ‾ ‾ ‾ ‾   ‾ ‾ ‾
a g v j c v   n c d q t   c p f

‾ ‾ ‾   ‾ ‾ ‾ ‾ ‾   ‾ ‾ ‾ ‾ ‾ ,
c t g   j g c x a   n c f g p

‾ ‾ ‾   ‾   ‾ ‾ ‾ ‾   ‾ ‾ ‾ ‾   ‾ ‾ ‾
c p f   k   y k n n   i k x g   a q w

‾ ‾ ‾ ‾ .   ‾ ‾ ‾ ‾ ‾ ‾   ‾ ‾ : ‾ ‾
t g u v   o c v v j g y   13 : 30

NEW INTERNATIONAL VERSION

‾ ‾ ‾ ‾   ‾ ‾   ‾ ‾ ,   ‾ ‾ ‾   ‾ ‾ ‾
e q o g   v q   o g   c n n   a q w

‾ ‾ ‾   ‾ ‾ ‾   ‾ ‾ ‾ ‾   ‾ ‾ ‾
y j q   c t g   y g c t a   c p f

‾ ‾ ‾ ‾ ‾ ‾ ‾ ,   ‾ ‾ ‾   ‾
d w t f g p g f   c p f   k

‾ ‾ ‾ ‾   ‾ ‾ ‾ ‾   ‾ ‾ ‾   ‾ ‾ ‾ ‾ .
y k n n   i k x g   a q w   t g u v

‾ ‾ ‾ ‾ ‾ ‾   ‾ ‾ : ‾ ‾
o c v v j g y   13 : 30

Thirty-four: Partner Points

Everyone in the class needs a partner. If there is an uneven number of students, the teacher can be a partner. Divide by counting one-two-one-two or pair older students with younger ones. The class has three minutes to attempt to learn the verse as partners. Then the fun starts.

The teacher points at one group and says one word in the verse. One of the partners must finish the verse from the word called out. If they can't do it, they lose two points. If they can, they gain five points. They then point to any other partnership and say one word from the verse. The chosen two must finish the verse, gaining or losing points. If the memory work is Psalm 1:1, the game might start with "Standeth" *(KJV)* or "Stand" *(NIV)*. Two-letter words and the, and, etc., should not be used. Nouns and verbs work best. The partners with the highest score at the end of the game are the champs.

As in all games of this kind, the teacher needs to be sure that everyone gets a turn.

Thirty-five: Peanut Hide

Make enough construction-paper peanuts to have one for each word in the verse times the number of students. Print the words of the memory verse on the peanuts, one word per peanut. Hide the peanuts before class, and at a given signal, the students hunt for the peanuts and put them in order in front of them. They will have to trade with friends to get the right words. After they have the peanut "verse" correctly in front of them, they must learn it. When they say the verse from memory, they can collect a real peanut or two.

KING JAMES VERSION

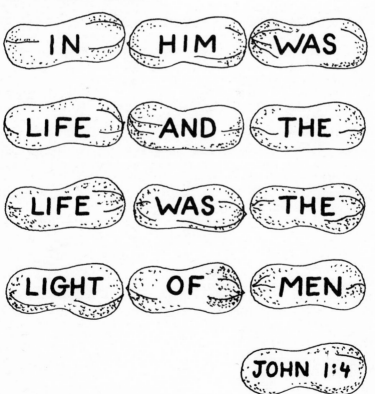

IN HIM WAS LIFE AND THE LIFE WAS THE LIGHT OF MEN JOHN 1:4

Thirty-six: One Shoe Off

Have all students remove one shoe and place them in the middle of the circle of students. After three minutes of practicing the verse for the day, a chosen person or the teacher picks out any shoe and proceeds to find the owner. If *it* finds the owner within thirty seconds, the owner must say the verse. If the owner isn't found in the time limit, *it* must say the verse. Then the owner can become *it* and find another shoe's owner. Continue the game until all have had an opportunity to say the verse.

KING JAMES VERSION

Thirty-seven: Picture Guess

For a verse that can be illustrated easily, "Picture Guess" is a good way of learning. Place pictures with no words on the flannelboard. Be sure the students associate each phrase with a specific picture. Test them by holding up a picture and having them say the phrase. Finally, let them "read" the verse by looking at the pictures. Ask for a volunteer to place the pictures on the board while he/she says the right words in order. Put the pictures away for a week or two. Then see if they can still "read" the verse. With a little peek into the Bible, they will remember for a long time.

NEW INTERNATIONAL VERSION

Thirty-eight: Bible Maze

Mysteries are fun. All ages enjoy them. Adapt a Bible verse into a mystery maze. The pencil must not cross a line as it finds the solution, then the mind must memorize the correct wording. It may help to make one large copy for the easel and small ones for the students. The copy machine will save many hours.

KING JAMES VERSION

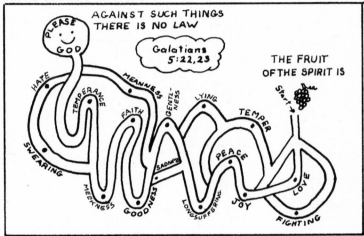

NEW INTERNATIONAL VERSION

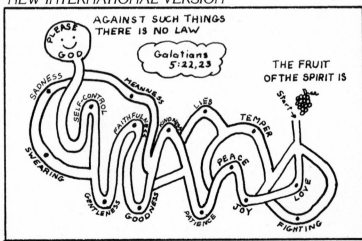

Thirty-nine: Clues in Blues

Clues in blues is an activity of enjoyment that leads to direct learning. The students must color all the blocks in the picture according to the color letter. The blue is all they need to remember. Example: Psalm 46:1

KING JAMES VERSION

choose R	praise Y	God B	hear G	is B
our B	over R	mark R	refuge B	clap Y
and B	people Y	strength B	a B	very B
present B	help B	shout G	in B	trouble B

NEW INTERNATIONAL VERSION

God B	choose R	is B	praise G	our B
hear Y	mark R	refuge B	over G	clap Y
and B	people R	strength B	an B	ever B
present B	help B	shout G	in B	trouble B

Forty: Cartoons

Most people love the comics. Save copies of Garfield, Peanuts, Fred Bassett, etc., until you have enough single cartoons for each class member. Cut out the captions and glue (or have the children glue) the cartoons onto white paper, then set the class to work. The rules are simple: 1) Write the verse of the day with the reference at the top of the paper. 2) Let the cartoon character explain the meaning of the verse in one sentence. 3) After five minutes, be ready to explain your cartoon to the class.

KING JAMES VERSION

NEW INTERNATIONAL VERSION

Forty-one: Color Me Brown

Make copies of your verses as shown below, and have the children color the pictures according to the color code. Tell them they should memorize only the words in brown. That makes it sound easy! A picture that illustrates the verse is a good way to go.

Color Code: BR = brown, R = red, B = blue, Y = yellow, O = orange

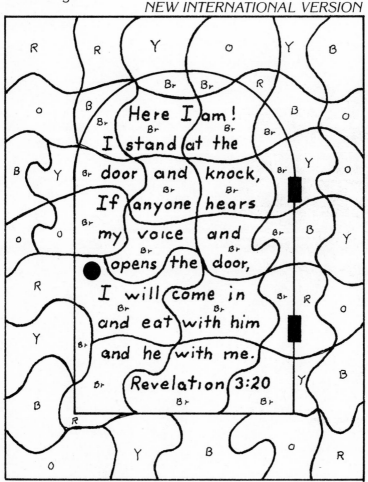

NEW INTERNATIONAL VERSION

Here I am! I stand at the door and knock, If anyone hears my voice and opens the door, I will come in and eat with him and he with me. Revelation 3:20

Forty-two: Magic Pyramid

A variation of the crossword puzzle, the pyramid is meant to cause thinking and learning. The puzzle may be presented as individual copies and the children work independently, or it may be made large enough for the class members to work together on it. With each word written into the pyramid, the children will be helped to remember the words. (Note: these are not the exact words of the verse.)

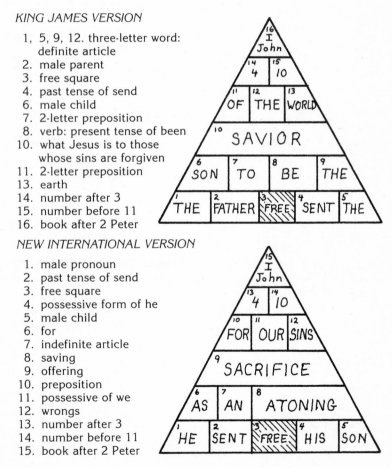

KING JAMES VERSION

1, 5, 9, 12. three-letter word: definite article
2. male parent
3. free square
4. past tense of send
6. male child
7. 2-letter preposition
8. verb: present tense of been
10. what Jesus is to those whose sins are forgiven
11. 2-letter preposition
13. earth
14. number after 3
15. number before 11
16. book after 2 Peter

NEW INTERNATIONAL VERSION

1. male pronoun
2. past tense of send
3. free square
4. possessive form of he
5. male child
6. for
7. indefinite article
8. saving
9. offering
10. preposition
11. possessive of we
12. wrongs
13. number after 3
14. number before 11
15. book after 2 Peter

50

Forty-three: Funny Dots

Prepare for each student a worksheet like the one below. Let them use colored pencils or felt pens to connect the dots to form words. After they have connected the dots, they must put the words in the correct order. Talk about the verse, read it aloud, then have the children say it from memory.

NEW INTERNATIONAL VERSION

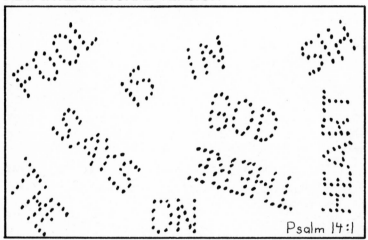

Forty-four: Quiz Whiz

There are many kinds of quizzes. This is meant to be a fast question-and-answer exchange. If it lags, it will lose its effectiveness. An enthusiastic teacher can, however, make it an exciting learning activity.

Rules: Answer before the teacher counts to five.
Answer correctly or sit one round in the penalty booth.
Bibles may be open (or the verse on the chalkboard) for the first round, closed for the second.
Using Proverbs 9:10, it might go like this:

1. Proverbs comes after what book? (Psalms)
2. What is the first word in the verse? (The)
3. What is the beginning of wisdom? (The fear of the Lord)
4. What is understanding? (The knowledge of the holy)
5. What is the reference? (Proverbs 9:10)
6. What word begins with F? (Fear)
7. What is the fear of the Lord? (The beginning of wisdom)
8. What word begins with U? (Understanding)
9. What is the knowledge of the holy? (Understanding)
10. What word begins with W? (Wisdom)
11. What is the second half of the verse? (The knowledge of the holy is understanding)
12. What is the second word? (Fear)
13. What word begins with K? (Knowledge)
14. Whom should we fear? (The Lord)
15. What is the last word? (Understanding)
16. What chapter is the verse in? (Ninth)
17. What word comes after wisdom? (And)
18. How many *thes* are there? (Four)
19. What is the fifth word? (Lord)
20. What word is the longest word? (Understanding)
21. What comes after understanding? (.)
22. The fear of the Lord is what? (The beginning of wisdom)

Forty-five: Finish the Fish

Make enough fish for each member to have one. Print the verse on the fish, cut it up in appropriate pieces (few for little ones, more for older learners), and set students to work. After they put the puzzle together, they must learn it. If they can't say it in three minutes, they should scramble their puzzle and do it again. Once they know the verse, they may glue it onto a large fish bowl as a review and reminder of the verse of the day.

KING JAMES VERSION

And he saith unto them, Follow me, and I will make you fishers of men. Matthew 4:19

NEW INTERNATIONAL VERSION

"Come, follow me," Jesus said, "and I will make you fishers of men." Matthew 4:19

Forty-six: Swell Bell

A cow bell, a Christmas bell, a ship's bell—whatever kind of bell you can lay your hands on—will work. Show it, ring it, let one child ring it, then put it up out of the way.

Tell the students to open their Bibles to the book of Matthew, chapter 24, verse 42. Wait until everyone finds it. (Help those who need it, especially new students and your slow learners.) Challenge them to memorize the verse before the bell rings. Count one, two, three, go! After two minutes, see who knows the verse. Let one who knows it perfectly be the bell ringer, giving the class another period of time, shorter than the first. The surprise factor makes the class work harder than usual.

KING JAMES VERSION NEW INTERNATIONAL VERSION

Forty-seven: Clothe the Verse With Words

Another way to make students think, or to make them hunt, is to let them work on the words as they subconsciously enter the mind. Memorization is then easier and better.

Draw a simple figure and let the first letter of each word appear with blanks for all of the other letters. These letters then become the clothing of the person. Use some boys, some girls. In the sketches below, the girl represents the KING JAMES VERSION and the boy represents the NEW INTERNATIONAL VERSION. After the letters are put on the correct lines, the students can learn it and say it to the teacher. The verse to remember is Isaiah 26:3.

Forty-eight: Around the Circle

The students form a circle and hold onto a strong string which is long enough to reach around the entire circle. The string is tied at the ends to make it continuous. Onto the string, before it is tied, place a ring with a verse attached to it. Ephesians 6:1, "Children, obey your parents in the Lord, for this is right," is a good verse to use.

The ring will be passed secretly in the fists of the students, from one person to another. *It* tries to guess who has the ring. If *it* guesses correctly, the one who has the ring must say the verse. If *it* is wrong, *it* must repeat the verse. After three or four times, remove the verse from the ring. Keep the game going about five minutes. Never let it go until it is boring. If the person caught can say the verse perfectly, he/she becomes *it*.

The string must be kept taut all the time, and students must keep both hands on it at all times to keep *it* guessing.

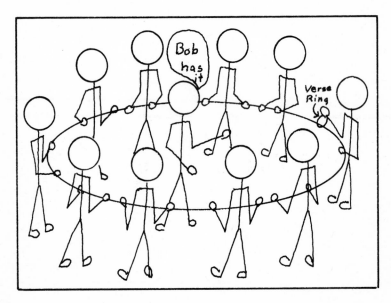

Forty-nine: Book Look

Give each child a 4″ x 6″ piece of paper. Have them fold the paper in half, then in half again, and cut the top fold to make a four-page book. The cover should bear the title, BOOK LOOK, and each page inside should have a phrase of the verse to be learned. Have the children draw a miniature illustration on each page to add to the understanding and the attractiveness of the booklet. The back page could have a hand-drawn or a stick-on star after the verse is memorized and a line for the teacher to sign when he/she is satisfied with the quote from the student. This booklet can go home to encourage further review and family participation.

NEW INTERNATIONAL VERSION

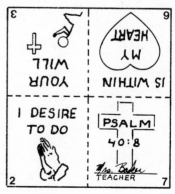

Fifty: Map the Trap

From an outline map, place the letters of the verse in a continuous line (no spaces) around the outline. At the end of the verse, add any miscellaneous letters to complete the map. Make enough copies of the map for each child to have one. They may underline the verse after they find it and learn it. When they know the verse, they may color the map and place a star where their hometown is located.

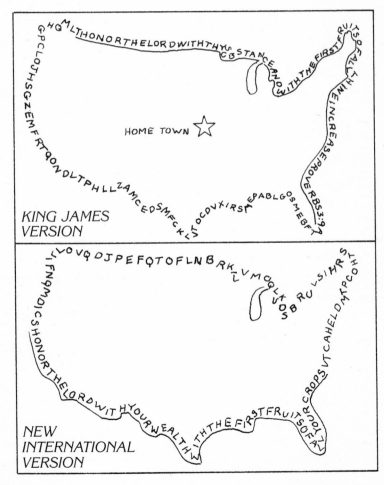

KING JAMES VERSION

NEW INTERNATIONAL VERSION

HOME TOWN ☆

Fifty-one: Dress the Mess

Most young people can relate to a mess: their rooms are sometimes a mess, a mud puddle makes their shoes a mess, their school papers often end up a mess. Today's Bible verse can cover a mess.

Give each student a paper person, and let him/her make it dirty, patched, and sad. Have pieces to put on the character that will teach the verse and its meaning. Appropriate verses are 1 Peter 2:16, Romans 13:14, Ephesians 4:24, and Colossians 3:10.

Each piece should be cut out and pasted over the messy character. When the student has dressed the mess, he should memorize the verse. Use the exercise to help students realize that sin must be confessed and forgiven, that God knows the heart, and that they should live for Him as His servants.

NEW INTERNATIONAL VERSION

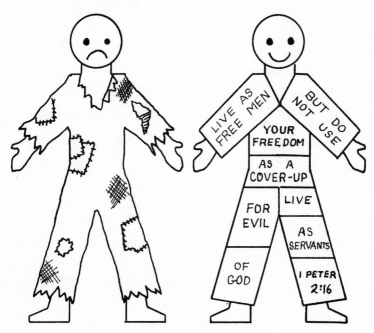

Fifty-two: Super Code

Most students like a mystery. This super code should stretch their minds and ready them for easier memorization. Each number represents a corresponding letter: 1 = A, 2 = B, 3 = C, 4 = D, etc. You may want to see if the children can discover the code without your help. If they can't, give them a hint: 5 = E. Wait several seconds, then say A = 1. If it is still beyond them, tell several other letters like 26 = Z, 24 = X. A longer verse should not be a problem to those in grades three and up. Try Acts 1:8.

KING JAMES VERSION

2 21 20   25 5   19 8 1 12 12   18 5 3 5 9

22 5   16 15 23 5 18 ,   1 6 20 5 18

20 8 1 20   20 8 5   8 15 12 25   7 8 15 19

20 9 19   3 15 13 5   21 16 15 14   25 15 21 :

1 14 4   25 5   19 8 1 12 12   2 5   23

9 20 14 5 19 19 5 19   21 14 20 15   13 5   2

15 20 8   9 14   10 5 18 21 19 1 12 5 13 ;

1 14 4   9 14   1 12 12   10 21 4 5 1 ,

1 14 4   9 14   19 1 13 1 18 9 1 ,

1 14 4   21 14 20 15   20 8 5   21 20 20 5

18 13 15 19 20   16 1 18 20 19   15 6   20 8 5

5 1 18 20 8   1 3 20 19 1:8

Fifty-three: Smiles

Gather the class into a circle. A student chosen to be *it* stands in the middle and selects another student to work with. The object is to get the person to smile. If he smiles, he must say the memory verse. For the first few times, have the verse on the chalkboard, then erase half of it, finally all of it. *It* cannot touch the person he is trying to make laugh. He can act funny, make funny noises, funny faces, imitate animals, etc. If the person doesn't smile in thirty seconds, *it* must try another student in the circle. The one who smiles and says the memory verse correctly gets to be *it*.

NEW INTERNATIONAL VERSION

Fifty-four: Doors

Make a large model of the doors below, and let the children copy it. Have various students open each of the doors, then close them and say the phrase. Finally, with all of the doors closed, have them say the verse. Verses adaptable to this method are numerous: Psalm 84:10, Genesis 4:7, 1 Corinthians 16:9, and the one illustrated here: John 10:9.

Fifty-five: Wiggle Jiggle

It is difficult and unnecessary for children to sit still for long periods of time. Halfway through the class, give them an opportunity to wiggle. During this time, they not only will learn a verse; they will be ready for the last half of the lesson. Ask the students to stand and say this little poem:

> WIGGLE IF YOU MUST,
> JIGGLE OFF THE DUST,
> WIGGLE AWAY THE RUST,
> JIGGLE YOUR _____ IN TRUST.

If the blank is arms, wave the arms high in the air while the class reads with the teacher the verse that is printed on the chalkboard. If the blank is toes, wiggle the toes while the verse is read. After five or six times, erase the board and continue the game until the verse is fixed in the minds of the students. You can add fingers, hands, knees, hair, shin bones, hips, neck, and elbows.

KING JAMES VERSION

Let the words of my mouth, and the meditation of my heart, be acceptable in thy sight, O Lord, my strength, and my redeemer. Psalm 19:14

Fifty-six: Tumble Tower

Use alphabet blocks (or let the children make them as a presession activity) for this exercise. Stack the blocks as shown below. Let the class read the verse. Remove one word and let the class say the verse. Remove another word, then another, etc. When the students have memorized the verse, remove a bottom block and the tower will tumble. One of the students who can say the verse perfectly can be the tumble-tower person. For review, let the students rebuild it correctly: last word first or first word last. Let a student choose another student to say the verse. If he/she cannot say the verse, the leader gets to tumble the blocks. If the student says the verse correctly, he/she gets to tumble the tower.

KING JAMES VERSION

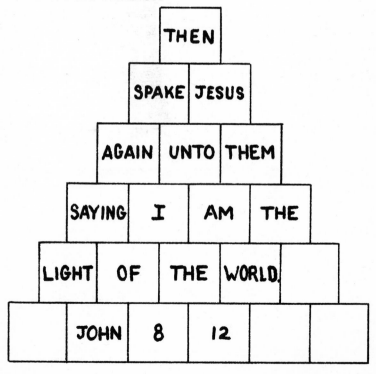

64

Fifty-seven: Overlaps

You will need three pieces of paper, 8½" x 22", for the teacher's visual. Each student will need three pieces of paper 4¼" x 11". Fold one sheet so that the top part is 4" long (8" for the teacher). This will be your first page. Fold the second sheet so that the top part (page 2 of your book) is 4¾" long (9½" for the teacher). Fold the third sheet so that the top part is 5¼" long (10½" for the teacher). This will be page 3. Staple the sheets together to make a book. Each extending page has a clue for the verse phrase on that page. When they have learned the verse, they may write it on the last page of the book.

KING JAMES VERSION

Fifty-eight: Petal Kettle

Make a kettle and some flower petals (as shown below) from construction paper. On each petal write a phrase from the memory verse, and add it to the kettle vase on the bulletin board as it is repeated. Soon the class will be able to say every word in order. You may want to let the students tack the petals to the bulletin board or remove them one at a time to test their fellow students. 2 Peter 3:18a works well with this method.

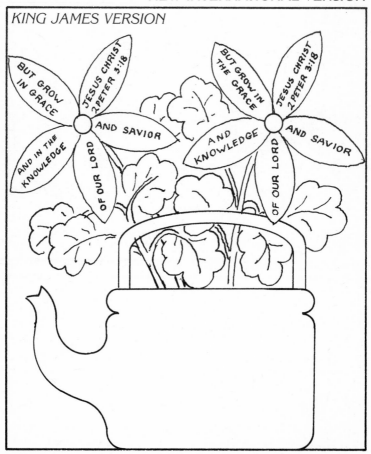

NEW INTERNATIONAL VERSION

KING JAMES VERSION

Fifty-nine: Continuous Words

Before class, draw a picture of Earth on one side of the chalkboard and Heaven on the other. Then, with the students watching, write the words in a continuous path (no spaces) from Earth to Heaven.

Students will remember the way the verse is presented, but more important, the words and their message will hit home as you read the words together.

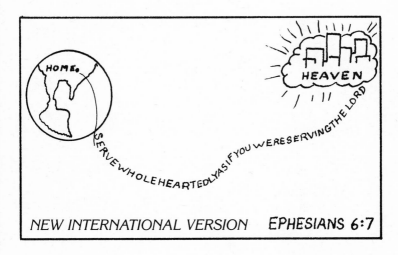

NEW INTERNATIONAL VERSION   EPHESIANS 6:7

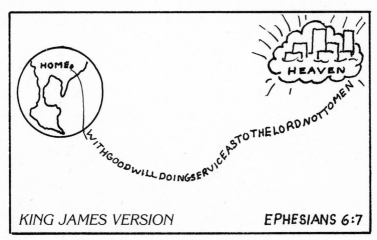

KING JAMES VERSION   EPHESIANS 6:7

Sixty: Button Find

Select a large button or make a cardboard button about 1½ inches in diameter. Print the verse on the button. Have one student hide the button while the others close their eyes. The button must be in plain sight, within the confines of the classroom. The students have thirty seconds to find it. If they can't find it, they must all say the Bible verse in unison. If one student finds it quickly, he/she may choose any student (or teacher) to say the verse from memory. No one person can be called on twice until everyone has been called on once. The finder gets to be the next one to hide the button. A neutral color is harder to find. Let it be hidden on a student, on the floor, on a piece of furniture, or whatever other place is chosen, as long as the students do not need to move anything to see it.

Sixty-one: Lines to Find

Write the words of the verse in random order on a piece of paper. Make a copy for each student.

With their Bibles open, the students draw lines to connect the words of the verse in the correct order. When a student is finished, he reads it several times until he can say it on his own. Another time, let each student figure out a review verse to hand over to a classmate and see if she can figure it out.

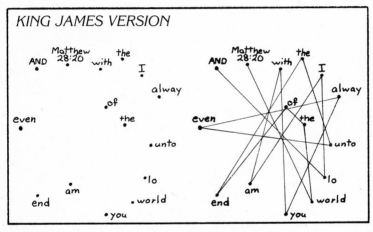

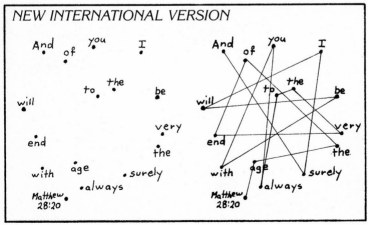

Sixty-two: Peek and Seek

"Peek and Seek" can be used in several ways. After the students have seen what is behind each window, have a guessing game. Use questions like these: Which number has a word beginning with *L* behind it? Which number has the word *whatever* behind it? Which number has a word beginning with *C* behind it? Which number has the Scripture reference? Which number tells us how to respond?

Try lifting half of the windows and see if the class can say the verse. Let a student open and close whatever windows he wishes and see if the class can say the verse.

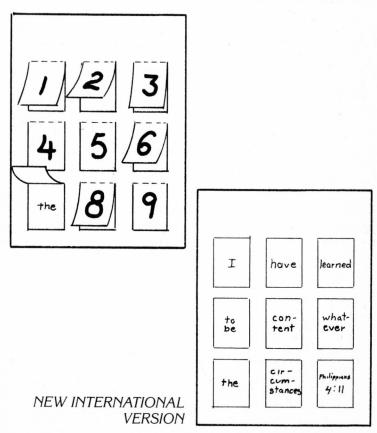

NEW INTERNATIONAL VERSION

Sixty-three: One Thought Leads

In this game, the teacher uses a series of questions to draw out the words of the verse from the class. To learn Psalm 62:8, it could go this way:

I need a word beginning with T.
A word that means believe.
A word with five letters.

TRUST

I need a word with two letters.
A preposition.
A word that begins with I.

IN

I need a pronoun.
A word to represent God.
A three-letter word.

HIM

I need a preposition.
A word that begins with A.
A word that shows time and place.

AT

I need a three-letter word.
A word that indicates total.
A word with two letters alike.

ALL

I need a word that means a span of days or years.
A plural word.
A word that begins with T.

TIMES

I need a two-letter word.
An old-fashioned word.
A word for you.

YE

I need a word for humans.
A word that begins with P.
A plural word without an S.

PEOPLE

I need a four-letter word.
A word that means to flow.
A word that begins with P.

POUR

I need a word that shows away from.
A word that has three letters.
A word that begins with O.

OUT

I need a word that is a form of you.
A word that has four letters.
A word that rhymes with more.

YOUR

I need a word that is a vital organ.
A five-letter word.
A valentine word.

HEART

I need a preposition.
A word that means in front of.
A word that begins with B.

BEFORE

I need a word that means God.
A pronoun.
A three-letter word.

HIM

I need a word for the Creator.
A word that has three letters.
A word that begins with G.

GOD

I need a short verb.
Part of the verb 'to be.'
A word that begins with I.

IS

I need a simple word.
A one-letter word.
The first letter of the alphabet.

A

I need a place of shelter.
A six-letter word.
A word that begins with R.

REFUGE

I need a preposition.
A three-letter word.
A word that rhymes with nor.

FOR

I need a word that means you and me.
A two-letter word.
A word that rhymes with bus.

US

The game may be played individually, on paper; on the chalkboard, by teams; or just the first one to know can call out his/her answer. With the complete verse before the students, give them three minutes to learn it and recite it. Another week, let the students figure out questions, assigning two words to each student.

Sixty-four: Envelope Secrets

There are several variations for this type of memory-verse game. I will suggest two ways to use it.

1. Inside each envelope, hide a word from the verse to be learned. Seal it and give one to each student. The students must line up according to the proper wording of the verse. As the verse is said by the class, each student rises as his word is said, then sits down again. In a few trials, the verse is memorized and the students have had fun in learning.

NEW INTERNATIONAL VERSION Psalm 143:10

2. Put part of a verse on the outside of the envelope. On the inside, place pieces of paper with the rest of the verse. Each student must open the envelope and figure out the rest of the verse in order to memorize it.

KING JAMES VERSION

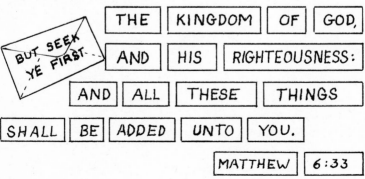

Sixty-five: One, Two, Three

At the count of three, the group must respond to the challenge of finishing the verse from the word the teacher calls out. At first, let the class answer together, with the verse visible to the class. Then call on individuals with the verse still visible. "Joan, one-two-three: Study." She must answer, "To shew thyself approved unto God. a workman that needeth not to be ashamed, rightly dividing the word of truth. 2 Timothy 2:15."

"And Bill, one-two-three: Workman." He should answer, "That needeth not to be ashamed, rightly dividing the word of truth. 2 Timothy 2:15." Finally, hide the verse and continue.

KING JAMES VERSION

One-two-three: *dividing*
One-two-three: *thyself*
One-two-three: *study*
One-two-three: *not*
One-two-three: *thyself*
One-two-three: *needeth*
One-two-three: *the*
One-two-three: *truth*
One-two-three: *God*

NEW INTERNATIONAL VERSION

One-two-three: *do*
One-two-three: *to*
One-two-three: *a*
One-two-three: *truth*
One-two-three: *present*
One-two-three: *workman*
One-two-three: *who*
One-two-three: *be*
One-two-three: *correctly*
One-two-three: *ashamed*

NEW INTERNATIONAL VERSION

Sixty-six: Ring Thing

Find an old ring-toss game, or make one. An old board with three dowel sticks fastened on will serve the purpose. Tape a piece of rope into a ring, or use the outer rim of a plastic cover. On the board beneath one dowel write, *5 points to say verse.* Under another, write, *10 points to say the verse and reference.* Under the third dowel write, *5 points to say the reference.* Give each student three rings and let them toss. Two teams will make it ever more interesting. Any verse may be used.

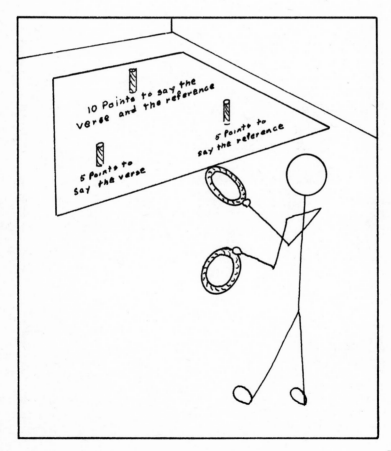

Sixty-seven: Bible Explorer

"Bible Explorer" is a board game that the teacher must make in advance. Equipment includes the board, made on a large piece of cardboard, squares and circles as shown on page 77, buttons or cardboard markers, and a spinner. Before the game is started, have the class say the verse together three times, then remove the verse. If a student makes a mistake, he/she may look at the verse once, take a forfeit, and wait until his/her next turn. If the verse is Luke 12:34, the game could be like this:

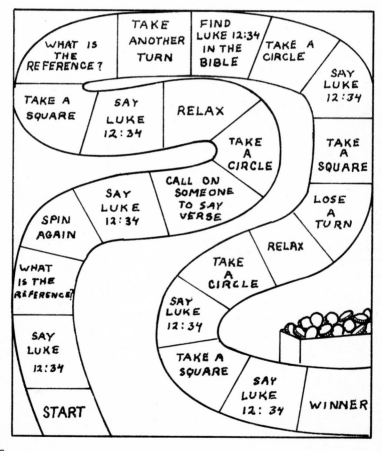

WHAT IS OUR TREASURE ?	WHERE WILL OUR HEARTS BE ?	WHO SAID THE WORDS IN LUKE 12:34?	WHAT IS THE FIRST WORD IN THE VERSE ?
WHAT DOES THE WORD HEART MEAN IN THE VERSE?	WHERE DO SOME PEOPLE PUT THEIR TREASURES ?	TO WHAT DOES ALSO APPLY IN THIS VERSE?	TO WHOM DID JESUS SAY THESE WORDS ?

WHAT IS THE LAST WORD IN THE VERSE?

WHAT CHAPTER IN LUKE HAS THIS VERSE?

WHAT DOES LUKE 12:34 MEAN TO YOU?

WHERE ARE WE TEMPTED TO PUT OUR TREASURES ?

HOW CAN YOU PUT YOUR TREASURE IN HEAVEN?

WHO WILL HELP YOU PUT YOUR TREASURE IN HEAVEN ?

WHICH TWO WORDS IN THE VERSE ARE MOST IMPORTANT ?

EXPLAIN LUKE 12:34 IN YOUR OWN WORDS.

GO FORWARD 1

GO BACK 1

GO FORWARD 2

GO FORWARD 2

GO FORWARD 4

GO FORWARD 3

GO FORWARD 2

GO BACK 1

Sixty-eight: Dare Chair

Arrange the chairs in a circle. Place a large sign on one chair and call it the DARE CHAIR. Announce, "When I clap my hands, everyone must change chairs. You may not sit in the same chair as you are in now." The student that ends up in the DARE CHAIR must say the Bible verse for the day. For the first five times, have the verse on the easel, then remove half of it for five times, then remove the entire verse and keep playing five more times. By then, all should be able to say the verse correctly.

KING JAMES VERSION

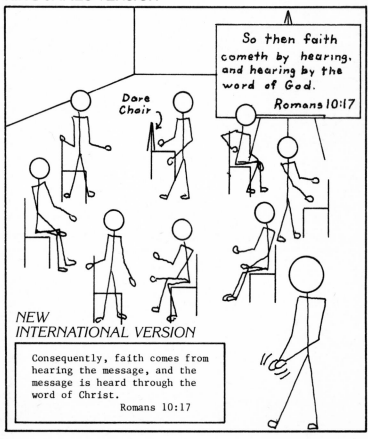

So then faith cometh by hearing, and hearing by the word of God.

Romans 10:17

NEW INTERNATIONAL VERSION

Consequently, faith comes from hearing the message, and the message is heard through the word of Christ.

Romans 10:17

Sixty-nine: Reverse Verse

Write out the verse vertically and from right to left as shown below. Make the letters large enough to be seen from across the room. Make a large cardboard triangle to cover part of the verse in the process of learning it. Then cover a different portion and see if the class can "quote the verse." Let one of the students come up and cover part of the verse with the triangle. Let someone who can say it perfectly hold the triangle over some of the words. Use the students often; it will make the lesson more meaningful.

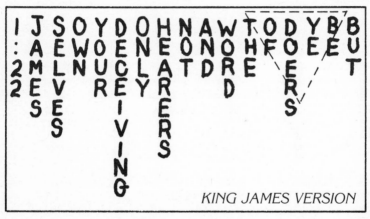

KING JAMES VERSION

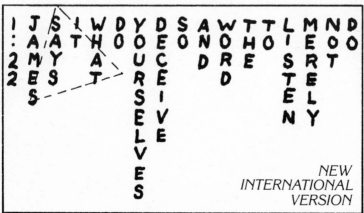

NEW
INTERNATIONAL
VERSION

Seventy: Secret Glasses

Write the verse to be memorized with only the vertical lines of the letters. On a piece of acetate or cellophane write only the horizontal lines of the letters. Place the cellophane over the paper to read the verse. The verse here is 1 Peter 4:9.

The children will enjoy doing this with other verses also.

OFFER HOSPITALITY TO ONE

ANOTHER WITHOUT GRUMBLING

I PETER 4 9

NEW INTERNATIONAL VERSION

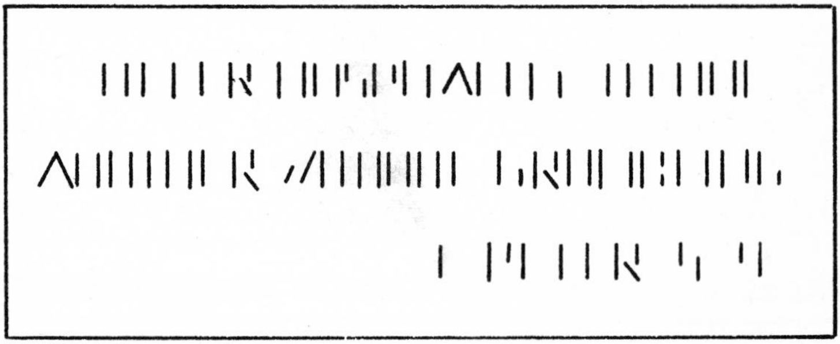

VERTICAL LINES

HORIZONTAL LINES

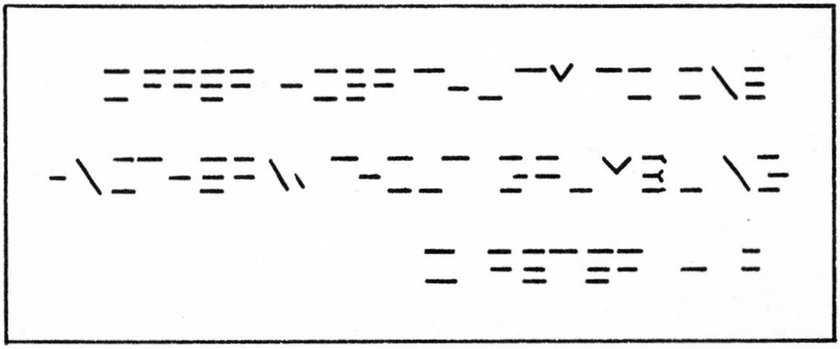

Seventy-one: Hunt Stunt

The object of this project is to hunt through the picture and find the words to the memory verse. Then the student may learn the verse. The picture can go home as a reminder. Any outline picture can be used to illustrate the verse; just eliminate a few lines, and insert words. As the students discover the words, they should write them in order to be sure they memorize the verse correctly.

NEW INTERNATIONAL VERSION

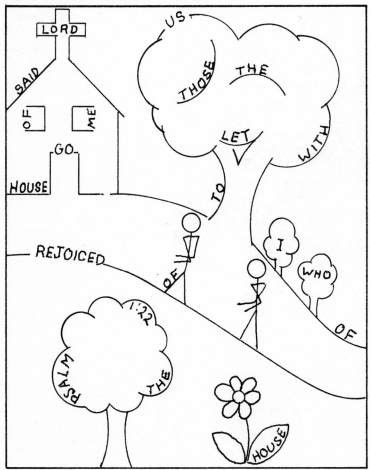

Seventy-two: Ten, Twenty, Plunge

"Ten, Twenty, Plunge" is a game; it is played in a circle with one person selected as *it*. *It* stands in the middle of the circle and points with his finger or a pointer at different classmates. He counts by tens around the group. He can count up as far as he wishes, by tens, but when he says "plunge," the student he points to must quote the verse chosen to be memorized. For the first five times, the verse may be on the chalkboard, then it should be erased and the students must say it from memory. If a student cannot say the verse, he becomes a third of a pickle. *It* should not pick on the same student until he has pointed to at least five other students. The teacher can change *it* as often or as seldom as she wishes. If the person who is *it* is slow, and makes the game boring, change in a couple of minutes. If *it* is enthusiastic and keeps the tempo high, you may want to let *it* be *it* for a longer time.

Seventy-three: Out of the Mix-up

Write out a verse with the words mixed up and no spaces between the words. Give each student a copy. As they work on the mix-up, give them a thirty-second glance at the verse on the chalkboard. Then they can work on straightening it out. They should cross out words as they put them into their solution. The exact number of blanks is provided in the solution form. After five minutes, they may use their Bibles to help with the solution. This is a long verse and may take two weeks for memorization. The second week, they may have the same puzzle with no Bible to help.

KING JAMES VERSION

IWHICHBYTHEREFORESERVICEBESEECHYOURY
OUUNTOBRETHEREN,REASONABLETHEBODIES
SACRIFICEACCEPTABLEHOLYGODMERCIESTHAT
OFYEYOURPRESENTGODISALIVE (Romans 12:1).

  ___ _____ _____ _____, _____,

_____ _____ _____ _____ _____, _____

_____ _____ _____ _____ _____

_____ _____, _____ _____ _____ _____

_____, _____ _____ _____ _____ _____

_____.

NEW INTERNATIONAL VERSION

IWORSHIPTHEREFOREURGESPIRITUALYOURBRO
THERSYOURSACRIFICESYOUVIEWWHICHPLEASIN
GINGOD'STOISHOLYANDBODIESOFMERCYLIVING
OFFERTOGODAS (Romans 12:1).

  _____, ____ _____ _____, _____ _____

_____ _____ _____ _____ _____, _____ _____

_____ _____ _____ _____ _____,

_____ _____ _____ _____—

_____ _____ _____ _____.

Seventy-four: Twirl

Let the students look at the verse for sixty seconds, then try to say the verse, one at a time. The student must stand on one foot and twirl as he/she says the verse. Because of the light nature of the activity, it would be better to have a light verse to learn with this method. If a student fails, he must sit down, study again, and await another turn. Some happy verses are James 5:11, John 13:17, and Proverbs 3:13. Don't worry if you cannot keep up with the students; they love to outdo the teacher!

NEW INTERNATIONAL VERSION

Seventy-five: Flipper Slipper

Make enough construction-paper slippers for each word of the memory verse. Place them in the center of a table in front of the students and let them read the verse in unison, and then individually. Quickly turn over one slipper, hiding the word you want, and see if the class can read the verse. Ask one student to read it. If he can, let him turn over another slipper. Then the class may say the verse again. Call on a student to say the verse alone. If he can, he can turn over still another slipper. Continue the process until the entire verse is upside down, thus completing the flipper slipper.

KING JAMES VERSION

NEW INTERNATIONAL VERSION

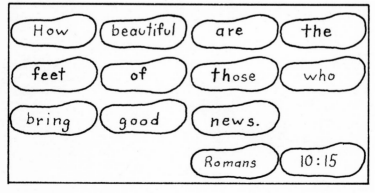

Seventy-six: Calendar Inspection

Have the students draw an appropriate calendar on 8½" x 11" paper for the current month. Have them write the days and the numbers in small characters, but leave large spaces for the verse they will add. Let them add cartoons to illustrate the verse, and a smiling face or a sticker once they know the Bible words from memory. Show them how to glue it on a three-sided holder to take home and refer to for a month of remembering. Psalm 90:12 is our example. Ephesians 5:16, Colossians 4:5, 2 Peter 3:8, and Hosea 10:12 are also appropriate for this project.

S	M	T	W	T	F	S
☺				1	2	3
4	TEACH 5	US 6	TO 7	NUMBER 8	OUR 9	10
11	DAYS 12	ARIGHT 13	THAT 14	WE 15	MAY 16	17
18	GAIN 19	A 20	HEART 21	OF 22	WISDOM 23	24
25	26	PSALM 27	90 28	12 29	30	31

MARCH

NEW INTERNATIONAL VERSION

To make a stand for the calendar, take a long piece of cardboard about 8" x 20" and fold it three times. Glue the two ends together, and the resulting triangle will make a stand.

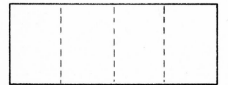

Glue

Seventy-seven: Color Land

Make copies of the verse to be learned in large block letters that the children may color with a marker or crayon. If the work is done on smooth paper, then pasted onto construction paper, it can be displayed in the class-room or taken home. For a "gloss" look, wrap the "framed" verse in plastic wrap and tape it on the back.

NEW INTERNATIONAL VERSION

Seventy-eight: Bugs Funny

Young people respond to funny things. Let each one make a funny bug on a 2" x 3" piece of construction paper. On the body of the bug, let them letter one word of the verse to be learned. On the back of each paper, let the children paste a piece of flannel paper. Then have them place their bugs on the flannelboard in the correct order. They can memorize the verse by saying it as a class. Have one student remove his bug while the class says the verse again. Continue the process until all the bugs are removed and the class can say the verse from a blank board.

Another time, let the students make enough bugs on their own 8½" x 11" paper to hold the words of the entire verse. They can print the words onto the bugs, cut them apart, mix them up, and put the words in order while they memorize it.

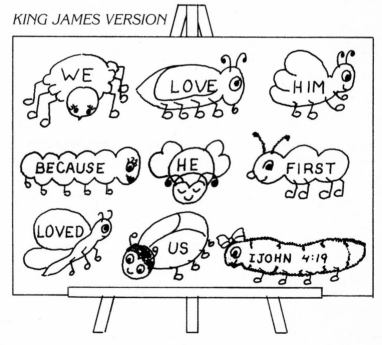

KING JAMES VERSION

WE LOVE HIM BECAUSE HE FIRST LOVED US IJOHN 4:19

Seventy-nine: Upside-down Folly

Have the students print the verse correctly in medium-size letters. Then, beneath each letter, they can repeat it, but upside down. The first several letters will go slowly, but they will gain ability after a word or two. Then they can cut off the right letters and try to memorize the words from the upside-down printing. Note the process below in our example: Luke 11:9.

KING JAMES VERSION

Eighty: Bible Addition

This method takes a little time to figure out a verse, but once the teacher has it on paper, she can use a copier and let each child figure out the verse, memorize it, and be delighted in the process. Mark 14:38 is our example.

W H A T – H + C H = __ __ __ __ __ __
Y O U – U + E – O = __ __ __
A L S O – S O + N – L + D = __ __ __ __
P R E T E N D – E T + A – E + Y – N D = __ __ __ __
L E T T E R – T + S – E – R = __ __ __ __ __
Y E L L – L – L = __ __ __
E R A S E – R + N T – A – S + R = __ __ __ __ __ __
I D L E – D + N – L E + T O = __ __ __ __ __
T I M E – I + E – E + P T + A T + I + O N =
__ __ __ __ __ __ __ __ __
T R O U B L E – R O – U – B L + H = __ __ __ __
S P R I N G – R I + I R – N + I – G + T = __ __ __ __ __ __ __
T O U G H – O + R – G H + L + Y = __ __ __ __ __ __
I N T O – N – T + S – O = __ __
R E A S O N – S + D – O N + Y = __ __ __ __ __ __
B U T T O N – T – O – N = __ __ __ __
T H I M B L E – I – M – B – L = __ __ __ __
F R I G H T E N – R + L – I G – T + S – N + H =
__ __ __ __ __ __
I L L – L – L + S = __ __ __
W A N T – A + E + A – N – T + K = __ __ __ __ __ __ *(KJV)*

W H A T – H + C H = __ __ __ __ __ __ __
A L S O – S O + N – L + D = __ __ __ __
P R E T E N D – E T + A – E + Y – N D = __ __ __ __
S I L L Y – I – L + O – L – Y = __ __ __
T H I N G – I + A – N – G + T = __ __ __ __ __
Y E L L – E + O – L + U – L = __ __ __ __
W O N D E R – O + I – N – D + L – E – R + L = __ __ __ __ __
N I C E – I + O – C – E + T __ __ __ __
F R I D A Y – R – D + L – Y + L = __ __ __ __ __
I D L E – D + N – L E + T O = __ __ __ __ __
T I M E – I + E – E + P T + A T + I + O N =
__ __ __ __ __ __ __ __ __ __
T R O U B L E – R O – U – B L + H = __ __ __ __
S P R I N G – R I + I R – N + I – G + T + __ __ __ __ __ __ __
I N T O – N – T + S – O = __ __
W R I T E – R + L + L – T + I – E + N + G =
__ __ __ __ __ __ __
B U T T O N – T – O – N = __ __ __ __
T H I M B L E – I – M – B – L = __ __ __ __
B U T – U + O – T + D + Y = __ __ __ __
I L L – L – L + S = __ __ __
W A N T – A + E + A – N – T + K = __ __ __ __ __ __ *(NIV)*

Eighty-one: Missing Screw

Boredom comes from the lack of preparation, from the same old thing, and from the "you learn it anyway" attitude. The missing screw is a fun puzzle that needs missing lines in each letter of the verse. Each child will need to add (draw in) screws to discover the verse.

Let them try it with Psalm 34:1.

NEW INTERNATIONAL VERSION

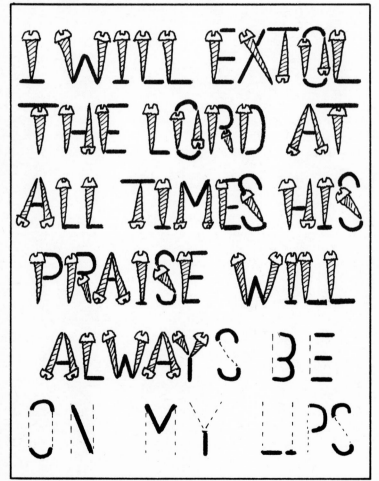

Eighty-two: Tear and Wear

A different process to try occasionally is the use of *tearing*. No project will be perfect, but what is accomplished may surprise both the teacher and the student. Choose a verse and think of an easy outline that will illustrate it. Then let the children tear it out, letter the verse words on it, and pin it on themselves when they can say the verse from memory. A straight pin works well.

Verses that are appropriate for this method are Matthew 6:28, Jeremiah 17:9, Romans 5:8, Matthew 28:6, and Mark 10:14.

KING JAMES VERSION

He is not here : for he is risen, as he said. Come, see the place where the Lord lay. Matthew 28:6

But when Jesus saw it, he was much displeased and said unto them,

Suffer the little children to come unto me and forbid them not;

for of such is the kingdom of God. Mark 10:14

Eighty-three: Bible Subtraction

This is an easy puzzle for most children. See if your class can do it in their heads rather than on paper. Little ones (first and second graders) should spell out the correct words before they proceed in the memory process. Any verse will work: just add an O or a ★ or a # or an X or a 1 or a & after every letter. See if they can "read" the verse and commit it to memorization. Here is how Psalm 92:1 looks when done this way.

Note: Subtract the extra letters or symbols and it becomes "Bible subtraction." The second example is easier than the first for younger ones.

KING JAMES VERSION

IOTO IOSO AO GOOOOODO
TOHOIONOGO TOOO GOIOVOEO
TOHOAONOKOSO UONOTOOO
TOHOEO LOOORODO AONODO TOOO
SOIONOGO POROAOIOSOEOSO
UONOTOOO TOHOYO NOAOMOEO OO
MOOOOSOTO HOIOGOHO.
POSOAOLOMO 9O2O:1O

NEW INTERNATIONAL VERSION

I&T& I&S& G&O&O&D& T&O&
P&R&A&I&S&E& T&H&E& L&O&R&D&
A&N&D& M&A&K&E& M&U&S&I&C&
T&O& Y&O&U&R& N&A&M&E& O&
M&O&S&T& H&I&G&H&.
P&S&A&L&M& 9&2&:1&

Eighty-four: Try or Cry

This is a time for acting. Let the old amateur clown burst forth and pretend to cry. Even have a box of tissues handy. Then teach the verse that goes with the lesson. Be brief, and expect some mistakes that will cause fun. The teacher can begin the process by pointing at a student and saying, "TRY or CRY."

If the student can say the verse, he points to another student and says, "TRY or CRY." When a student makes a mistake or can't say the verse, the rest of the class must "CRY." The teacher does the pointing unless the student says the verse perfectly. That helps to keep the action moving and gives everyone a chance or two. The comics will emerge, laughter will be more prevalent than tears, and memorization will result.

Suppose Proverbs 20:1 is the verse. It can be done this way: "Bob, TRY or CRY!"

Note: Always be careful not to embarrass students who may be younger or slower than the others.

NEW INTERNATIONAL VERSION

Eighty-five: Under the Rug

The Bible verse to be memorized is written on a large paper for all to see. After saying it five times, place it under a light rug on top of a table. Have the students say the verse together. They may peek if they need to. Then call on someone to say the verse. Anyone who has to peek gets five points. Keep going around the class (not necessarily in order) until every student has had two chances. The students with the least number of points are the winners.

Eighty-six: Say It Again

Write the verse on the board for all to observe for the first several minutes, then remove it. Say the verse in a loud clear voice. Then tone it down a little, then a little more, until, finally, you are whispering. The last time, just mouth the words. Then let the students say it in this way with the teacher. After this, each student should know the words from memory and be able to say the verse in a normal tone.

NEW INTERNATIONAL VERSION

Eighty-seven: Bean-bag Time

Cut several shaped holes on one side of a cardboard box and label them as follows: "5 points, today's verse," "10 points, last week's verse," "5 points, today's reference," "3 points, any verse." Place the box ten feet from the starting line. Each student gets three chances to try to throw a bean bag through a hole, and do what the label says.

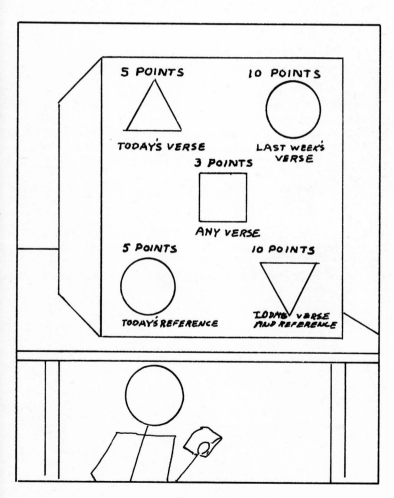

Eighty-eight: Idea Trap

A mental game, "Idea Trap," is fun for thinking students. The teacher should be the spokesperson for a while, then as the students understand the rules and the pace of the dialogue, they can be it. The game involves a series of questions and answers. If the verse to be memorized is Jeremiah 33:3, it could go like this.

Note: For the first few times, have the verse in front of the students, then remove it for memory's sake.

NEW INTERNATIONAL VERSION

It: The idea trap has caught you. *(Point to student.)*
Student: Who, me?
It: Yes, you.
Student: Why me?
It: To see if you know the words that come after *GREAT.*
Student: And unsearchable things you do not know. Jeremiah 33:3.
It: The idea trap gives you ten points. And it has caught you. *(Point to another student.)*
Student: Who, me?
It: Yes, you.
Student: Why me?
It: To see if you know the words that come after *ANSWER.*
Student: Me and tell me....
It: Sorry, the idea trap doesn't accept that. It takes five points away from you, and the idea trap has caught you. *(Point to another student.)*

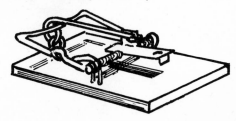

Eight-nine: String Along

A string, long enough to go around the students at the table or standing in a circle, is needed. On a plastic cover from a food container, print with a permanent marker the verse for the day. Punch a hole in the cover, place the string through it, and tie the ends of the string. All students must place their hands on the string. They pass the lid from student to student, as fast or as slow as they desire, but it must keep moving. When the music stops, or when a bell is sounded, the student caught with the lid must say the verse. For the first five times, they may read it from the lid. Then they must remember the words without looking. If a child can't say the verse, he becomes a third of a knot. Try to keep anyone from dropping out of the game. If they do, they usually don't learn the verse and don't enjoy the game. Within a ten-minute period, the entire class should be able to say the verse from memory.

Ninety: Stick Lick

Write the verse of the day on some gummed paper, then cut it in puzzle fashion: many pieces for older students, few pieces for the little ones. Have them first put it together on the table, then, when they have it placed correctly, have them stick it on a background paper. This makes a good take-home project or a bulletin-board display. After a student puts the verse together, have him/her say the words to the teacher. A last activity before going home can be a review of the verse of the day. If it goes home, it will be another reminder.

KING JAMES VERSION

NEW INTERNATIONAL VERSION

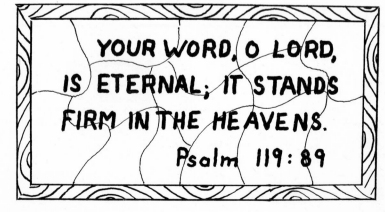

Ninety-one: Bible Multiplication

As soon as students are into multiplication in school, that knowledge can be used in memorization. Assign a number to each letter of the alphabet and let the children work out an arithmetic page. The answers will be their verse to memorize. If the verse is 1 Corinthians 10:31 it would look like this:

A=2   B=4   C=6   D=8   E=10

F=12   G=14   H=16   I=18   J=20

K=5   L=15   M=25   N=35   O=45

P=55   Q=65   R=9   S=21   T=27

U=33   V=36   W=39   X=42   Y=48

Z=51   C O D E

```
 13      4     10      9      8      5      3
×3     ×4     ×1     ×3     ×2     ×2     ×3
───    ───    ───    ───    ───    ───    ───
 39
 W     ───    ───    ───    ───    ───    ───


  3      4      2      3     10      6      5      1      5
×9     ×4     ×5     ×3     ×1     ×2     ×9     ×9     ×2
───    ───    ───    ───    ───    ───    ───    ───    ───

───    ───    ───    ───    ───    ───    ───    ───    ───


 24      5            10      1      3                    5      3
×2     ×2            ×1     ×2     ×9                    ×9     ×3
───    ───           ───    ───    ───                  ───    ───

───    ───           ───    ───    ───                  ───    ───


  4      3      2      7      5             9      9
×2     ×3     ×9     ×5     ×1            ×5     ×1
───    ───    ───    ───    ───           ───    ───

───    ───    ───    ───    ───           ───    ───


 13      8      2      9      3      9      5     12     10      9
×3     ×2     ×1     ×3     ×7     ×5     ×2     ×3     ×1     ×1
───    ───    ───    ───    ───    ───    ───    ───    ───    ───

───    ───    ───    ───    ───    ───    ───    ───    ───    ───


 12      5             4     45             2      5
×4     ×2            ×2     ×1            ×4     ×9
───    ───           ───    ───           ───    ───

───                  ───    ───           ───    ───


  2      5      3             9      5             9      8      5
×1     ×3     ×5            ×3     ×9            ×3     ×2     ×2
───    ───    ───           ───    ───           ───    ───    ───

───    ───    ───           ───    ───           ───    ───    ───


  7      5      9      9     12             5      4
×2     ×3     ×5     ×1     ×4            ×9     ×3
───    ───    ───    ───    ───           ───    ───

───    ───    ───    ───    ───           ───    ───


  7     45      8
×2     ×1     ×1          KING JAMES VERSION
───    ───    ───

───    ───    ───  .
```

102

Ninety-two: The Missing Word

Make copies of verses with missing words for all the students. Let the students find in their Bibles the missing words, then memorize the verse. After a child memorizes the verse, he can then devise this verse or another verse in a different way and let his/her friend solve it.

KING JAMES VERSION

The next _____ John _____ Jesus

coming _____ him, _____ saith,_____

the _____ ___ ____,

which _____ _____ the _____ of

the _____. John 1:29

NEW INTERNATIONAL VERSION

The next _____ John _____ Jesus

coming _____ him _____ said, "_____,

the _____ ___ ____

who _____ _____ the _____ of

the _____." John 1:29

103

Ninety-three: Feather Guide

Make some construction-paper feathers of different colors. Make a headband as shown below. The object is to get all of the feathers on the headband, even if it takes some players longer than others. Let the students number off and take turns. Keep the verse on the board for the first five minutes.

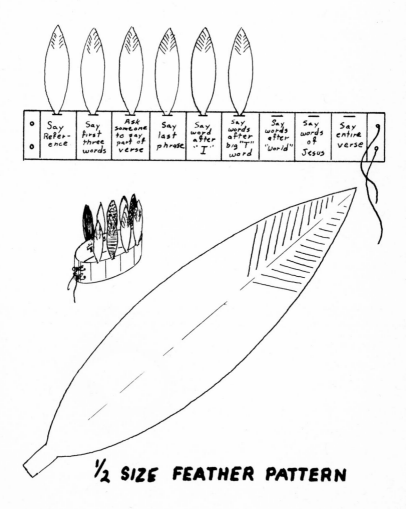

	Say Reference	Say first three words	Ask someone to say part of verse	Say last phrase	Say word after "I"	Say words after big "T" word	Say words after "World"	Say words of Jesus	Say entire verse	

½ SIZE FEATHER PATTERN

Ninety-four: Bible Search

"Bible Search" is a word game that will be fun for anyone old enough to read and count. Even adults will have fun with this. The students must find each word by looking up Bible verses, counting to the right word, and writing it on the paper. Finally, he/she will memorize the verse that is already partially fixed in the mind. Give a time limit, according to age, for the game.

Our example is Ephesians 2:8.

KING JAMES VERSION

1. First word in Luke 9:24 _____

2. Fourth word from end in Matthew 13:21_____

3. Eighth word in 2 Corinthians 9:8 _____

4. Second word in Luke 6:21 _____

5. Eighth word of John 3:7 _____

6. Fourth word from end in Acts 16:31 _____

7. Fifth word from end in Romans 5:1 _____

8. Third word in Romans 10:17 _____

9. First word in Acts 15:1 _____

10. Fifth word from end in Mark 3:2 _____

11. Eleventh word of Matthew 4:4 _____

12. Seventh word in Mark 3:35 _____

13. Second word in John 3:28 _____

14. Second word in Mark 4:4 _____

15. Ninth word of Mark 4:11 _____

16. Second word in Romans 6:23 _____

17. Eleventh word of John 4:10 _____

18. Sixth word in Luke 3:1 _____

19. Last word in John 1:1 _____

NEW INTERNATIONAL VERSION

1. First word in Luke 9:24 _____

2. First word in Ephesians 4:11 _____

3. Third word in John 17:20 _____

4. Seventh word in Romans 5:2 _____

5. Eighth word in 2 Corinthians 9:8 _____

6. Third word in 1 Corinthians 11:2 _____

7. Second word in John 17:6 _____

8. Third word in Matthew 5:31 _____

9. Twelfth word in Acts 16:31 _____

10. Seventh word in Romans 5:1 _____

11. Second word in Romans 10:17 _____

12. First word in Luke 18:6 _____

13. Second word in John 1:19 _____

14. Next to last word in 1 Corinthians 13:4 _____

15. Ninth word in Galatians 3:2 _____

16. Second word in John 3:28 _____

17. First word in Mark 1:2 _____

18. Fourth word from end in Mark 4:11 _____

19. Second word in Mark 14:12 _____

20. Eighth word of John 4:10 _____

21. Fifth word of Galatians 3:26 _____

22. Twelfth word of John 1:1 _____

Ninety-five: Another Hangman

This variation will keep the class using their brains. Instead of guessing letters for the word, they must guess words for the verse. Before each guess, the leader can give a simple clue like this:

One word begins with S.
One word rhymes with side.
One word is the past tense of do.
One word ends with T.
One word is a connecting word (conjunction).
One word is a preposition.

With each mistake, a part of the person is added to the gallows until the entire figure is drawn. These are the steps in drawing: HEAD, BODY, ONE LEG, ANOTHER LEG, ONE ARM, ANOTHER ARM, ONE FOOT, ANOTHER FOOT, ONE HAND, ANOTHER HAND, ONE EYE, THE OTHER EYE, NOSE, MOUTH, HAIR, ONE EAR, THE OTHER EAR. The first time the game is played, the teacher should be the leader. The next time (not the next Sunday) let a student be the leader.

King James Version

> If ye abide in me, and my words abide in you, ye shall ask what ye will, and it shall be done unto you.
> John 15:7

107

Ninety-six: Take a Plane

All ages—young children, older children, teens and adults (that's right, adults!)—like to make paper airplanes. Use the desire rather than letting it be a disrupting incident.

Give everyone a piece of paper, 8½" x 11" or 5" x 7". In five minutes, everyone must make an airplane that will fly, and the memory verse must be inscribed on the fuselage. Then line up the students at one end of the room. The owner of the plane that travels farthest calls on another student to recite the verse. The one who is second, calls on another student. It keeps going until all have said the verse. If they still don't know the verse, give them thirty seconds to modify their planes and try again, going through the same process of saying the verse. Perhaps this time, in order to win, the owner of the farthest plane must quote the verse to get credit; if he can't, number two wins.

NEW INTERNATIONAL VERSION

Ninety-seven: Catch the Train

Each student will make one car of a long train. If there are more words than students, let faster-working students make a second car. Each car must have a word of the Bible verse on it. Then the cars are to be hitched together with a paper clip. A string can be tied to the engine, and the train can be moved around the table top while the students say the verse over and over again. While they are learning it, move the train slowly. Once they know the verse, move the train faster and faster. It will prove they know it if they can repeat the words while the train is moving too quickly for them to read the words on the cars. Finally, place the train on the bulletin board for review.

Ninety-eight: Bible Division

From third grade onward, division is not difficult. It will be fun to figure out, and it will be easy to memorize once the student has figured out the answers. The process can be worked for any verse, and copies can be made for each student. Set a time limit. To avoid embarrassment, divide in teams of two, pairing slower students with faster students.

Our example is Psalm 51:4a.

Code for *New International Version:*

A=26	B=25	C=24	D=23	E=22
F=21	G=20	H=19	I=18	J=17
K=16	L=15	M=14	N=13	O=12
P=11	Q=10	R=9	S=8	T=7
U=6	V=5	W=4	X=3	Y=2
Z=1				

A   G __ __ __ __ __

26   20

$2\overline{)52}$ $5\overline{)100}$ $2\overline{)52}$ $3\overline{)54}$ $2\overline{)26}$ $8\overline{)64}$ $4\overline{)28}$

__ __ __ ,   __ __ __

$2\overline{)4}$ $3\overline{)36}$ $6\overline{)36}$ $4\overline{)8}$ $4\overline{)48}$ $4\overline{)24}$

__ __ __ __ ,   __ __ __ __

$3\overline{)36}$ $2\overline{)26}$ $3\overline{)45}$ $8\overline{)16}$ $3\overline{)57}$ $4\overline{)104}$ $3\overline{)15}$ $4\overline{)88}$

__   __ __ __ __ __ __

$5\overline{)90}$ $2\overline{)16}$ $3\overline{)54}$ $2\overline{)26}$ $3\overline{)39}$ $2\overline{)44}$ $4\overline{)92}$

__ __ __   __ __ __ __

$4\overline{)104}$ $3\overline{)39}$ $2\overline{)46}$ $3\overline{)69}$ $2\overline{)24}$ $4\overline{)52}$ $3\overline{)66}$

__ __ __ __   __ __

$3\overline{)12}$ $2\overline{)38}$ $3\overline{)78}$ $3\overline{)21}$ $2\overline{)36}$ $5\overline{)40}$

__ __ __ __   __ __

$2\overline{)44}$ $5\overline{)25}$ $2\overline{)36}$ $3\overline{)45}$ $3\overline{)54}$ $3\overline{)39}$

__ __ __ __

$6\overline{)12}$ $3\overline{)36}$ $6\overline{)36}$ $3\overline{)27}$

__ __ __ __ __ .

$4\overline{)32}$ $2\overline{)36}$ $5\overline{)100}$ $2\overline{)38}$ $2\overline{)14}$

Ninety-nine: Five Alive

The class must sit in a circle (around a table or in an open space). The teacher can begin the game. She counts as she points to students in order. "One, two, three, four, five alive!" The student who is five alive must stand and say, "Must I strive?" "Yes, into the verse you must dive!" At that instruction, the student must repeat the chosen verse. If he can, he can start anywhere in the circle and count off, "One, two , three, four, five alive!" and the number five answers, "Must I strive?" If the student cannot answer with the verse, the leader responds, "Enough said, you're one-third dead!" And she begins counting again with the person next to him. For the first five times, have the verse printed on the chalkboard. Then erase it and let the students remember it from memory.